LIFE'S BEST GPS EVER!

FINDING YOUR WAY IN THIS COMPLEX WORLD

SUSAN STIVER

RLS CREATIVITY PUBLISHING

Scripture taken from THE MESSAGE. Copyright © 1993, 1994, 1995, 1996, 2000, 2001, 2002. Used by permission of NavPress Publishing Group.

Scripture quotations taken from the (NASB®) New American Standard Bible®, Copyright © 1960, 1971, 1977, 1995, 2020 by The Lockman Foundation. Used by permission. All rights reserved. lockman.org

All photos taken by Susan Stiver unless otherwise noted.

E-Book ISBN: 978-1-998542-15-4

Paperback ISBN: 978-1-998542-14-7

Cover Design by John Bryll Pulido johnbryllpulido@gmail.com

Interior Design by RLS Creativity Publishing ruthlsnyder@me.com

Published 2025 by RLS Creativity Publishing P.O. Box 7562, Bonnyville, AB T9N 2H8

CONTENTS

Dedicated to Don,

My husband, my best friend this side of heaven,

My travel companion, my compass, my map-man.

He taught me how to enjoy the journey.

To our children, grandchildren, and great-grandchildren

Teach the next generation the joy of traveling,
and map reading,
so, they will never be lost.

PREFACE

Some people will pick this book up to read, but never finish – that's like having a map, and tearing pages out, or pieces off. Or maybe you'll have a poor signal for your GPS when you need it the most. I hope that's not you. Stay the course so you don't miss some places you may need to visit, or may want to go experience in the future.

My husband and I have had the privilege of seeing all 50 of these beautiful United States – mostly on the back roads. Forty of those states were experienced riding on a Honda Valkyrie motorcycle – two wheels in the wind. What an adventure! We are grateful for the markers and milestones God has given us as we traveled this Journey called Life. Some of those markers are places we've been, things we've seen, people we've met along the way – both in the natural and supernatural realm. Markers are also emotional extremes, turning points, intersections, right and wrong decisions, dead-ends, U turns, stop and go signs, and navigating through storms. Am I talking to anyone out there, or is this all for me? I encourage you to stay the course, read on - you may find a part of your own journey in these pages.

Carlsbad, CA

I'll write the book on Your righteousness,
talk up Your salvation all the day long,
never run out of good things to write or say.
I come in the power of the Lord God,
I post signs marking His right-of-way.

You got me when I was an unformed youth,
God, and taught me everything I know.
Now I'm telling the world Your wonders;
I'll keep at it until I'm old and gray.
God, don't walk off and leave me
until I get out the news
Of Your strong right arm to this world,
news of Your power to the world yet to come,
Your famous and righteous ways, O God.
God, You've done it all!
Who is quite like You?

Psalm 71:15-19 (The Message)

❧

Be strong; show what you're made of!
Do what God tells you.
Walk in the paths He shows you:
Follow the life-map absolutely,
Keep an eye out for the signposts,
His course for life set out in the revelation to Moses;
Then you'll get on well in
Whatever you do and wherever you go.

I Kings 2:2-3 (The Message)

❧

For new drivers, experienced drivers, and those who are recklessly driving through life ignoring the signs, here's a GPS to consider. It's the best map and set of directions ever to be found! Illuminating the path, it will lead, but not nag you. The choice to follow it is up to you.

Just as road signs help us reach our destination,
GPS – GOD Posted Signs
are available to help us reach our destiny!

Life is exciting! Enjoy the journey!

THE JOURNEY BEGINS

DAY 1

"Drivers start your engines!" That works for Nascar, but life is not a race to see who gets to the finish line first. Let's make this a "Sunday Drive". In this fast pace world, some people may not know what that phrase means. A "Sunday Drive" is like taking a leisurely stroll through a park – someplace away from the hustle bustle of the city. A place where you can stop and smell the flowers - without being run over. So much is missed on the dog-eat-dog interstates. Jump off the expressways, and experience the back roads. Take in the local culture. Stop for a snack at a Mom and Pop diner.

Drive far enough away from the big cities, and you may discover trails to explore with waterfalls and streams to dip your toes in on a warm afternoon. These wonderful places are out there, but you can't be in a hurry, or you'll miss the treasures to be found.

See you on the open roads!

ROAD TESTED

DAY 2

What a God! His road stretches straight and smooth.
Every God-direction is road-tested.
Everyone who runs toward Him makes it.

Psalm 18:30

～

Ever gone somewhere and the road turns to gravel then dirt? If you're like me that usually happens when I'm running late, and have decided to take a short cut. Sometimes it's my failure to plan well. I thought I knew the way so I didn't recheck the map before I left. Other times there's unexpected road construction. Either way it's time to regroup and come up with Plan B. Anxiety heightens as the road grows more narrow without a driveway in sight for turning around. Revert to training – the dreaded three-point turn.

～

More than three maneuvers later – success! Headed back to the pavement, I am relieved when I finally feel smooth road under the tires. Safely rolling again I am reminded that God's road stretches straight and smooth. Running toward Him, my destination is sure.

SIGN POSTS AND CROSSROADS

DAY 3

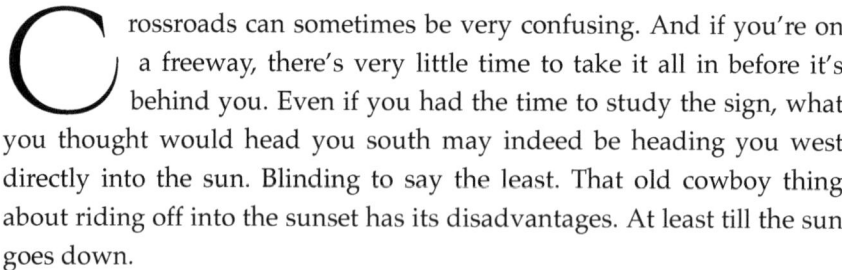

The signposts of God are clear and point out the right road.
The life-maps of God are right, showing the way to joy.
The directions of God are plain and easy on the eyes.

Psalm 19:7-9

Crossroads can sometimes be very confusing. And if you're on a freeway, there's very little time to take it all in before it's behind you. Even if you had the time to study the sign, what you thought would head you south may indeed be heading you west directly into the sun. Blinding to say the least. That old cowboy thing about riding off into the sunset has its disadvantages. At least till the sun goes down.

Life is full of crossroads and turning points. Places where decisions have to be made as to what direction we will take. There's not always time to stand there on the corner to consider the options. Studying the life-map daily will help prepare us for the road ahead. I'm so grateful that the directions of God are plain and easy on the eyes.

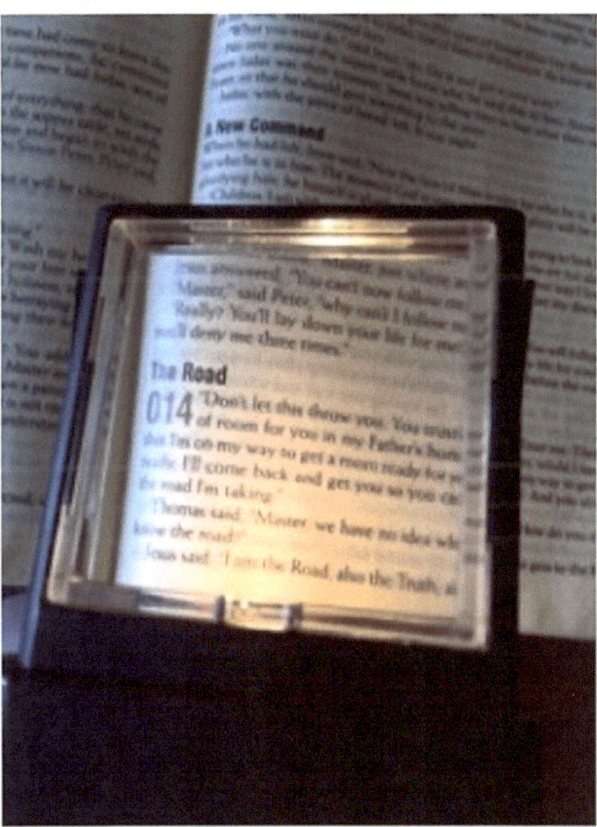

John 14

CROSSROADS
CAFE
Breakfast Lunch Dinner
Beer Wine Cocktails

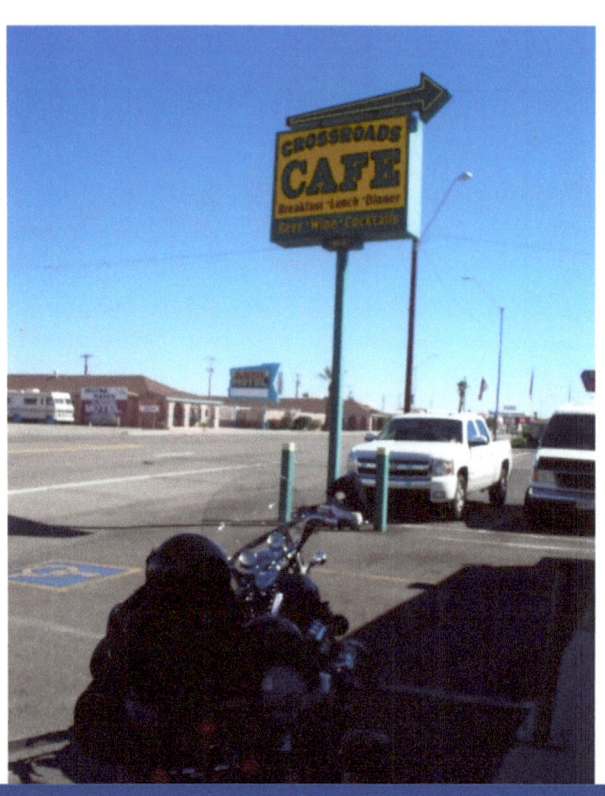

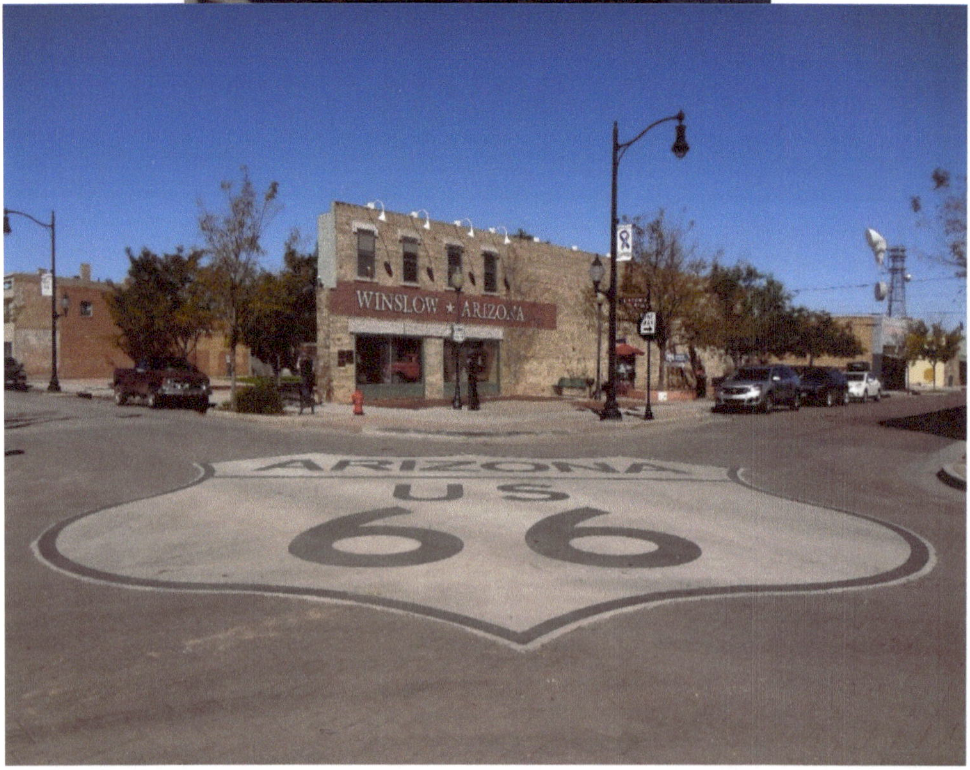
WINSLOW ★ ARIZONA
ARIZONA
US
66

I've brought you today to the crossroads of Blessing and Curse.
The Blessing: if you listen obediently to the commandments of God,
your God, which I command you today.
The Curse: if you don't pay attention to the commandments of God,
your God, but leave the road that I command you today,
following other gods of which you know nothing.
Deuteronomy 11:26-28

MAKE THE U TURN

DAY 4

Mark the milestones of Your mercy and love God;
Rebuild the ancient landmarks!...
God is fair and just; He corrects the misdirected,
Sends them in the right direction...
From now on every road you travel
Will take you to God.
Follow the Covenant signs,
Read the charted directions.

Psalm 25:6, 8, 10

~

S ounds almost like a trip to the slammer, and through the legal system. Incarceration stops a person in his/hers tracks, but prison isn't just a physical place with iron bars and bolted doors. Mental and spiritual bondage can lock a person up in a hopeless pattern of defeat. Truth be known, this can be a very strategic point. Like hitting a wall at a hundred miles an hour – the pain is tremendous, but somehow still alive, one realizes that there is another direction. God meets people at the wall. "God is fair and just; He corrects the misdirected, sends them in the right direction." It's up to the person at the wall to receive the mercy and love of God and then to turn around and move toward God. He sets us on a course toward freedom. Make the U Turn.

TRAVEL THE WELL-LIT STREET

DAY 5

Point me down Your highway, God;
Direct me along a well-lighted street.

Psalm 27:11

~

Some people can see well in the dark, or so they say. If they were truly honest, probably nine out of ten of them would admit to stubbing their toes at least once. Even at dusk when shadows are long it's easy to misstep and stumble. Now let's add travelling in a car into the mix. Driving is nearly impossible without any light. Dusk is difficult enough, but then comes night. Sudden dense fog is a danger all its own. Headlights from oncoming traffic are not always a welcome sight.

~

With all that, it becomes apparent just how crucial proper lighting is for the journey. Two important elements of life are the right road with the right light – God's highway and God's Light. With God as our map and our light, our journey is sure. He makes the way clear.

YOUR LANTERN AND COMPASS

DAY 6

Give me Your lantern and compass, give me a map,
So I can find my way to the sacred mountain,
To the place of Your presence,
To enter the place of worship, meet my exuberant God,
Sing my thanks with a harp,
Magnificent God, my God.

Psalm 43:3-4

Hand me a compass and I am lost; a map without an indicator as to where I am on that map, and I am still lost. Shed some light on the subject and I can see that I am really lost.

I am delighted that the world does not revolve around me. It is only by God's lantern and His compass with His map that I am able to find my bearings on the earth. By His design my destination is the sacred mountain, the place of His presence. Come with me and there we will meet our exuberant God and worship Him with our thanksgiving hearts. How magnificent is our God!

STOP!

DAY 7

Step out of traffic!
Take a long, loving look at Me, your High God,
Above politics, above everything.

Psalm 46:10 (The Message)

∽

Be still and know that I am God.

Psalm 46:10 (NAS)

∽

S TOP signs require us to be still. How long depends on the traffic at the intersection. STOP is not meant to be a mere suggestion. There is a reason for this type of sign. If rolled, there could be an accident. Take the time to ascertain that the road is clear. If ignored, it could cost you a ticket or worse your life and the lives of others. A high price to pay!

Did you know that God waits at intersections all throughout our day? He waits between night and morning, morning and afternoon, afternoon and evening, evening and nighttime. He doesn't hold up a sign. He just lovingly waits to meet us. Be still and you will find Him – even better, you'll get to know Him!

KEPT OUT OF THE DITCH

DAY 8

Bless our God, O people!
Give Him a thunderous welcome!
Didn't He set us on the road to life?
Didn't He keep us out of the ditch?
He trained us first,
passed us like silver through refining fire,
Brought us into hard scrabble country,
Pushed us to our very limit,
Road-tested us inside and out,
Took us to hell and back;
Finally brought us to this well-watered place.

Psalm 66:8-12

B aha! An off-road trip through the desert will certainly push any one to their limit. All terrain road-tested – is there such a thing? Some roads are rougher than off-road trails. By the end of the ride you know what you're made of – more resilient than you knew! Our Guide set us on the road to life, but He is so gracious not to leave us stranded in a ditch out in the middle of nowhere. He has promised to bring us to a well-watered place – a place of abundance. Don't give up along the way. Push through to the promise.

NAVIGATE THROUGH THE DETOURS

DAY 9

Oh, dear people, will you listen to Me now?
Israel, will you follow My map?

Psalm 81:13

❦

Google maps and MapQuest have not always been reliable. Unexpected road construction and detours can reroute you for miles. One missed turn can add hours to a trip. And don't you just love it when you finally stop to ask directions the answer is, "You can't get there from here."?

❦

Sometimes we arrive in the wrong place because we didn't listen to the directions or we failed to follow the map. Determine to pay close attention to the voice of the Guide, and to follow His map. He can even help you navigate through the detours.

DON'T VEER OFF
DAY 10

Don't veer off to the right or the left.
Walk straight down the road God commands
so that you'll have a good life
and live a long time in the land that you're about to
possess.

Deuteronomy 5:32-33

REMEMBER THE WILDERNESS

DAY 11

Remember every road that God led you on
for those forty years in the wilderness,
pushing you to your limits,
testing you so that he would know
what you were made of...

Deuteronomy 8:2

~

Trust Him to go with you, and to take you through the wilderness times.
The journey will make you stronger.

FOLLOW/LIVE A GOOD LIFE

DAY 12

So now Israel, what do you think God expects from you?
Just this: Live in his presence in holy reverence,
follow the road he sets out for you,
love him, serve God, your God,
with everything you have in you, obey the commandments
and regulations of God that I'm commanding you today—
live a good life.

Deuteronomy 10:12-13

SEE YOU AT THE TOP

DAY 13

And how blessed all those in whom You live,
Whose lives become roads You travel,
They wind through lonesome valleys, come upon brooks,
Discover cool springs and pools brimming with rain!
God-traveled, these roads curve up the mountains
and at the last turn -
Zion! God in full view!

Psalm 84:5-7

∾

Our lives being the highways that God travels – what an interesting thought. As we have read, God puts us on this road to life. His desire is that we would choose to travel with and towards Him. Yes, the roads moves through some pretty desolate valleys, but even there we can find cool springs and refreshing pools. From there it's upward to the mountains – to the high and holy mountain – the place of His presence. He created us for Himself. There is no greater traveling companion, or desirable destination. See you at the top!

WALK STRAIGHT

DAY 14

Train me, God, to walk straight;
Then I'll follow Your path.

Psalm 86:11

~

Babies, when they learn to walk, wobble and tumble more than they walk. Some revert to crawling. Sailors develop what they call "sea-legs" to help them keep their balance as the ship is tossed and pitches on the open seas. Intoxicated individuals can seldom see straight, much less walk straight. Those of us who can walk still stumble on occasion and deviate from the straight path.

~

Each of us, whether we are willing to admit it or not, needs to be trained by God to walk straight. It is only by yielding to our Father and listening to His directions that we are able to follow His true path. That's part of growing up.

SAFE PLACE

DAY 15

Some of you wandered for years in the desert,
Looking but not finding a good place to live,
Half-starved and parched with thirst,
Staggering and stumbling, on the brink of exhaustion.
Then, in your desperate condition, you called out to God.
He got you out in the nick of time;
He put your feet on a wonderful road
that took you straight to a good place to live.

Psalm 107:4-9

～

The Israelites wandered forty years in the desert. How about you? What was your wilderness experience? I believe each of us has at least one – a time when there were no words to describe your pain whether physical or emotional; when there were words, but there was no one to listen or care; when depression was so heavy you could see no end; when loneliness was so deep you knew no one would understand; when the whole world was your

enemy and you felt like an army of one. Have you ever been that isolated and desperate?

There's good news! It only takes one call and it doesn't even require a phone. Cry out to God! He hears and He's our ever present help in time of trouble. He will get you out in the nick of time, and put your feet on a wonderful road.

STAY THE COURSE

DAY 16

You are blessed when you stay on course,
Walking steadily on the road revealed by God.
You're blessed when you follow His directions,
Doing your best to find Him.
That's right - you don't go off on your own;
You walk straight along the road He set.

Psalm 119:1-3

~

Have you ever headed out and never made it to your destination? When people travel their goal is usually to get where they're going. To do that they need to stay on course. Now what if you're traveling with a group? Is staying on course important? Emphatically, YES! If any one person should stray off on their own, the travel would be hindered and the safety of the group could be compromised. There is value to following directions.

There is even more value to following God's directions. "You are <u>blessed</u> when you stay on course… You're <u>blessed</u> when you follow His directions…" We are encouraged to do our best to find God. In finding Him we are blessed beyond anything we could ever imagine. He is our destination.

KEEP YOUR EYES ON THE ROAD

DAY 17

Be generous with me and I'll live a full life;
Not for a minute will I take my eyes off Your road.
Open my eyes so I can see
What You show me of Your miracle-wonders.
I'm a stranger in these parts;
Give me clear directions.

Psalm 119:17-19

~

P eople can't go a long time without blinking, especially when driving. Has the blink ever caused you to miss the turn? Have you been in a place where the locals say, "You ain't from around here, are ya?" Or been so powerful turned around that it sure would be nice to have some clear directions? Convenient stores aren't all that convenient, and directions from locals may be more detail than you can grasp. "Well, you go up to the Doctor's house on the hill... the one where they did the drug bust... You got any room in your car?" So you've been through Keokuk?

Stop, take a deep breath. Maybe it's time to grab a bite to eat at a local diner. Collect your thoughts, then pursue your journey refreshed.

BARRICADE IN THE ROAD

DAY 18

Barricade the road that goes Nowhere;
Grace me with Your clear revelation.
I choose the true road to Somewhere,
I post Your road signs at every curve and corner.
I grasp and cling to whatever You tell me;
God, don't let me down!
I'll run the course You lay out for me
If You'll show me how.

Psalm 119:29-32

～

M ost, if not all, people do not set out to end up Nowhere. Yet there are times when the road runs out either to a dead end, or bridge out. Not exactly what we hoped for as a destination. Life is full of choices. We can stay there and pout, or rant and rave, but we are still there – Nowhere. A better alternative is to turn around and head back – at least we're moving. What we do on our way back is most important. Do we just wave at others as they head toward the same dead end, or do we try to flag them to stop or post warnings so they can modify their travel plans? Wouldn't we have appreciated a barricade?

What's so wonderful is that God will post barricades for us if we ask AND pay attention to His GPS. Help us grasp whatever You tell us, Father.

A STONE IN THE ROAD

DAY 19

Careful! I've put a huge stone on the road to Mount Zion,
a stone you can't get around.
But the stone is me! If you're looking for me,
you'll find me on the way, not in the way.

Romans 9:33

S ometimes God puts obstacles in our life to protect and redirect us. Watch for those kinds of signs, and know that there's a better way.

TRAVELING THE FREE-WAY

Guide me down the road of Your commandments;
I love traveling this freeway!

Psalm 119:35

~

T raveling the freeway can be related to speed, but it can also be freedom in the journey. When are people the most free? When they are doing the right thing. Sounds simple, doesn't it – so why don't we do it?

~

Starts as a small child challenging the rules. Parents slowed children down with timeout in the corner. Schools created a method to address misbehavior – after school detention. Lots of things slow us down in life. Little white lies turn into bigger dark lies that detain our brains as we try desperately to remember all the other half-truths that lead up to this one. Driving over the speed limit may cause us to be detained by a law officer with a ticket book in hand. Red lights detain us at on ramps for the free-way, but if ignored it could mean being detained in a hospital or worse.

Life's travel can be smoother if we always choose the FREE-way.

ANCIENT LAND MARKS

DAY 21

I watch for Your ancient landmark words.
And I know I'm on the right track.

Psalm 119:52

L andmarks help travellers get their bearings. Think about the roads you travel the most. Familiar buildings, shops, parks, and houses all remind you that you are on the right road, in the right neighborhood. Just as physical structures help us get our bearings, so too, words keep us headed in the right direction. Not just "right", "left", "up", "down", "north", "south", but words like "love", "hope", "faith", and "peace" help us keep our feet on the ground and our lives moving in a positive direction.

Does that mean the road will always be smooth, and we travel without bumps and ruts? No, but when there is hope, the journey is not over. So, with expectancy we look for the landmark words that revive and strengthen us for the road ahead.

WORDS OF LIGHT

DAY 22

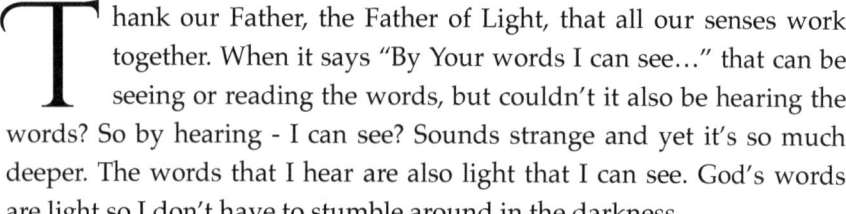

By Your words I can see where I'm going;
They throw a beam of light on my dark path.

Psalm 119:105

❧

T hank our Father, the Father of Light, that all our senses work together. When it says "By Your words I can see..." that can be seeing or reading the words, but couldn't it also be hearing the words? So by hearing - I can see? Sounds strange and yet it's so much deeper. The words that I hear are also light that I can see. God's words are light so I don't have to stumble around in the darkness.

Lots of people walk around in darkness even at midday because they never turn on the light. They never open the Book that could shed light on all their circumstances. They never go to the Father of Light for His counsel or direction. Many have never known, and others have forgotten, how to find their way to the light. If you know the way, share it with those who have never known, and remind those who have forgotten. God has promised that He will be found if we seek Him with all our heart.

FIND THE GOOD TRAILS

DAY 23

So now you can pick out what's true and fair,
find all the good trails!
Lady Wisdom will be your close friend,
and Brother Knowledge your pleasant companion.
Good Sense will scout ahead for danger,
Insight will keep an eye out for you.
They'll keep you from making wrong turns,
or following the bad directions
Of those who are lost themselves
and can't tell a trail from a tumbleweed,
These losers who make a game of evil
and throw parties to celebrate perversity,
Traveling paths that go nowhere,
wandering in a maze of detours and dead ends.

Proverbs 2:9-15

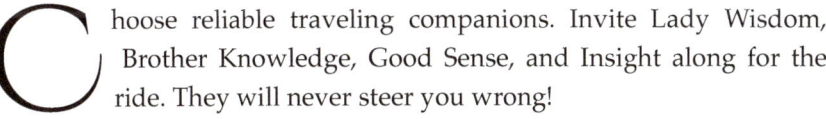

C hoose reliable traveling companions. Invite Lady Wisdom, Brother Knowledge, Good Sense, and Insight along for the ride. They will never steer you wrong!

WATCH THE ROAD SIGNS

DAY 24

Dear friend, take my advice; it will add years to your life.
I'm writing out clear directions to Wisdom Way,
I'm drawing a map to Righteous Road.
I don't want you ending up in blind alleys,
or wasting time making wrong turns.
Hold tight to good advice; don't relax your grip.
Guard it well—your life is at stake!
Don't take Wicked Bypass; don't so much as set foot on
that road. Stay clear of it; give it a wide berth.
Make a detour and be on your way.
The ways of right-living people glow with light;
the longer they live, the brighter they shine.
But the road of wrongdoing gets darker and darker—
travelers can't see a thing;
they fall flat on their faces.

Proverbs 4:10-15, 18-19

Watch the road signs – take the ones that lead to light, wisdom and right-living. Beware of the Bypass. You may end up on the wrong side of town, trapped in a blind alley. Move towards the light. The way will be clear and the road open for adventure. You must choose.

LEAD ME ON LEVEL GROUND

DAY 25

Point out the road I must travel;
I'm all ears, all eyes before You.

Psalm 143:10 (The Message)

❧

Teach me to do Your will, for You are my God;
Let Your good Spirit lead me on level ground.

Psalm 143:10 (NAS)

❧

S ometimes people refer to life as an "uphill battle". Things don't go the way we thought they should, so we work hard at trying to "fix it". We push, pull, and shove obstacles and people as if it were our job to make everything all right. Exhausted and spent we pause to evaluate our progress only to discover that we are no further along than when we started. Fact is, we may have even lost ground. Depressed and despondent it's easy to give up, but there's something better we can do. Stop trying! Our Father wants us to listen and watch. He'll tell us, and show us, how to proceed through this life. It's up to Him to set things right. Pull into the Rest Area. Wait and watch with a thankful heart.

READ THE MAP

DAY 26

How can a young person live a clean life?
By carefully reading the map of Your Word.
I'm single-minded in pursuit of You,
Don't let me miss the road signs You've posted.

Psalm 119:9-10

∽

L ife is full of signs. Signs tell us where we are, what to expect up ahead, and when the road changes direction. With symbols and words we know to merge, yield, slow down, or stop. By color we are alerted to impending danger – yellow for caution, red requiring immediate response or attention.

∽

Life is also full of maps – city maps, state maps, national maps, world maps. None of these help us a bit without one important key. Signs and maps are meant to be READ! Unless they are read and understood we will never reach our destination.

Yes, life is full of signs and maps. Guaranteed the best map you'll ever read is God's Word and the best GPS you'll ever find are God Posted Signs!

DON'T GET OFF TRACK

DAY 27

So, no matter where you are on your journey...
Don't get off track, either left or right,
so as to make sure you get to where you're going.

Joshua 1:7

THE CHOICE IS YOURS

DAY 28

In all your ways acknowledge Him,
And He will make your paths straight.

Proverbs 3:6 (NAS)

The choice is yours!
I challenge you to explore God's Word to locate even more
God Posted Signs.

YOUR LIFE IS A JOURNEY
DAY 29

Your life is a journey you must travel with a
deep consciousness of God.
It cost God plenty to get you out of that dead-end,
empty-headed life you grew up in.
He paid with Christ's sacred blood, you know.
He died like an unblemished, sacrificial lamb.
And this was no afterthought.
Even though it has only lately—at the end of the ages—
become public knowledge,
God always knew he was going to do this for you.
It's because of this sacrificed Messiah,
whom God then raised from the dead
and glorified, that you trust God,
that you know you have a future in God.

I Peter 1:18-21

As Solomon blessed Israel, I bless you with his words:
Blessed be God,
who has given peace to His people Israel
just as He said He'd do.
Not one of all those good and wonderful words
that He spoke through Moses has misfired.
May God, our very own God, continue to be with us
just as He was with our ancestors -
may He never give up and walk out on us.
May He keep us centered and devoted to Him;
following the life path He has cleared,
watching the signposts,
walking at the pace and rhythms He laid down
for our ancestors...
Then all the people on earth will know
God is the true God; there is no other God.
And you, your lives must be totally obedient to God,
our personal God,
following the life path He has cleared,
alert and attentive
to everything He has made plain this day.

I Kings 8:56-58, 60-61

TRAVELER'S BLESSING

DAY 30

May God our Father Himself and our Master Jesus
Clear the road to you!
And may the Master pour on the love so it fills your lives
and splashes over on everyone around you, just as it does
from us to you. May you be infused with strength and
purity, filled with confidence in the presence of God our
Father when our Master Jesus arrives
with all His followers.

I Thessalonians 3:11-13

Needles Highway

T hough the way may be narrow – even then there are signs to alert us of potential danger.

FOG = FAVOR OF GOD

DAY 31

For it is You who blesses the righteous man, O Lord,
You surround him with favor as with a shield.

Psalm 5:12 (NAS)

~

God can bring us home in the fog.
FOG = Favor of God

CROSS COUNTRY PHOTOS

TRAVEL LIGHT

P hotos of Our Cross-Country Rides taken in 2007 and 2010

Lake Saint Mary in Glacier State Park - View from Highway to the Sun

Travel light. Go with expectancy and great joy!
The road awaits your arrival.

~

Happy Trails!

~

ALSO BY SUSAN STIVER

- He Loves You to Pieces
- A Heart Stirred for Fellowship (Co-authored with her husband Don Stiver)
- A Walk in the Garden (Go Beyond Me - Book One)
- The Ebb and Flow of Life and Family (Go Beyond Me - Book Two)
- There's Always More: A Journey to Self-Discovery (Go Beyond Me - Book Three)

Contact the Author:

Susanstiver212@gmail.com

ABOUT THE AUTHOR

Susan Stiver is a storyteller, artist, and lifelong adventurer—equal parts backyard explorer and bold motorcycle rider. From climbing trees as a child to capturing breathtaking landscapes on camera, she has always followed the signs that pointed to wonder.

Her journeys—by car, train, plane, and prayer—have led her across physical miles and spiritual milestones. Along the way, Susan discovered that every road holds a story, and every story holds a glimpse of God's heart.

Today, she weaves those discoveries into words and brushstrokes, inviting readers to see the world as she sees it: full of beauty, mystery, and divine direction. Her passion is to reflect the love of God through writing and art—reminding each traveler that they are fully seen, deeply known, and lovingly guided.

The world is bursting with God-wonders. Come along—and see for yourself.

www.ingramcontent.com/pod-product-compliance
Lightning Source LLC
Chambersburg PA
CBHW040847120626
46547CB00001B/62